The How I Met Your Mother Cookbook

Recipes Inspired by The Legen-Wait-For-It-Dary Show!

BY: DAN BABEL

Copyright © 2020 by Dan Babel

License notes

No part of this publication or its contents may be copied, printed, published, or distributed by any means without the express permission of the author. This book is bound by copyright law, and the author reserves all rights to its publication. While the author has done the required research to ensure that all contents are accurate enough to inform and instruct, the reader is responsible for its content consumption. The author shall not be held accountable to anyone for damages resulting from the text being misinterpreted.

Table of Contents

Introduction 6

Prosciutto Melon 8

Seared Scallops with Mango Chutney 10

Lobster Ravioli with Black Truffle Oil 12

The Best Burger In New York 16

Gazola's Pizza 19

Hummus with Veggie Sticks 23

Nachos with Tomato Salsa 26

Mac and Cheese 28

Pumpkin Risotto 31

Marshall's Cheese Board 34

Stir Fried Chicken Noodles 37

Chicken Dumplings 40

Buffalo Wings 44

Sumbitches Cookie 47

Victoria's Cupcakes/Cake 50

Carrot Cupcakes 53

Chocolate Brownie with Strawberries.. 56

Thanksgiving Turkey 60

7-layer Erickson Inspired Salad 64

Baked Gouda in Potato Skin 67

Salmon Sushi.. 70

Meatball Sub sandwiches 73

Beef Teppanyaki... 76

Vegan Spring rolls 79

The Robin Scherbatsky 82

The Stinson's Hangover Fixer Elixir 84

Thankstini 86

The "Thank You, Linus" 88

Marshall's Self-Love Daiquiri 90

The Yellow Umbrella... 92

Robin's "But-um" shots 94

Conclusion 96

Author's Afterthoughts 97

About the Author 98

Introduction

How I Met Your Mother, ah, the memories that I have watched that show! I discovered HIMYM when I was in college and this sitcom became a respite from all those dreadful assignments!

The characters in HIMYM are as varied as the food that appears in the show. From Lily with her fantastic culinary skills, to Ted with his turkey stuffing ideas, to Marshall and his cheeseboard, the show covers a wide range of dishes… There's something for every level of cook in this show!

If you are an advanced cook, you will enjoy Lily's Prosciutto Melon or even the Scallops with Mango Chutney. On the other hand, if you love a scotch old enough to order its own scotch, the drinks in this book will hold a tremendous appeal! And if you are secretly an Erikson at heart, the 7-layer salad with heaps of bacon and mayo will definitely get your stomach rumbling!

Well, what are you waiting for? Let's jump right in, it's time to be legen-wait-for-it-dary, LEGENDARY!!

Prosciutto Melon

This is one of Lily's fancier dishes. However, it is super simple to make. The sweetness of the melon is an absolute delight with the prosciutto and the mint and balsamic glaze provide that perfect balance. I can't wait for you to try this swanky entrée!

Serves: 4

Time: 20 mins

Ingredients:

- 1 Musk melon or Cantaloupe, cut into wedges
- 12 Thinly sliced prosciutto
- 2 tbsp Honey
- 2-3 Mint leaves, Few leaves chopped
- Baby arugula or any salad greens, 1 bunch or handful
- Balsamic glaze, Some to drizzle

Method:

Peel the melon and deseed it. Cut through into halves and then into wedges. One melon should yield 10 to12 wedges.

In a bowl, take 2 tablespoons of honey, add some chopped mint leaves to it.

Marinade the melon wedges in this mixture by tossing it thoroughly. Leave it for some time to infuse all the flavors to the melon.

Take the slices of prosciutto and wrapped it to the melon wedges.

Arrange the prosciutto wrapped melons on a platter.

Place some baby arugula in the center of the arranged melons.

Drizzle with some balsamic reduction and serve cold.

Seared Scallops with Mango Chutney

Another one of Lily's fancier recipes, that sounds so much more complicated than it actually is. The only trick here is not to cook the scallops for too long. As soon as they have a nice golden-brown crust on them, take them off the heat!

Serves: 2

Time: 30 mins

Ingredients

- 8 Scallops (without the roe)
- 2 cups semi-ripe mango, diced
- ½ cup Sugar
- Salt and pepper, To taste
- ½ teaspoon Fennel seeds
- 2 Lemons
- Few sprigs Parsley, chopped
- 3 tablespoons, Olive oil

Method:

Mango chutney:

Take a pan and lightly caramelize the sugar. Add the diced mangoes to it and stir.

Add some salt and cook the mangoes till it releases the water on low heat. Add a cup of water and the fennel seeds and cover it. Cook it for around 15-20 minutes on medium heat till the mangoes are soft and chutney thickens. Leave aside to cool.

Scallops:

Marinate the scallops in salt, pepper, olive oil and lemon juice on a plate,

Heat a non-stick pan on high heat. Add some olive oil and sear the scallops on the heated pan.

Sear the scallops for a minute on both sides until a golden crust appears.

Serve the seared scallops with warm or cold mango chutney and lemon wedges on side.

Lobster Ravioli with Black Truffle Oil

It doesn't get any fancier than this! Reserve this dish for a fancier occasion because it isn't a cheap one to make. Having said that, it does taste spectacular, and will blow the minds of anyone you're trying to impress!

Serves: 4

Time: 3 hours

Ingredients

For the filling:

- 2 Lobster big
- 3 tablespoon Onions finely chopped
- 1 tablespoon Garlic finely chopped
- 1 ½ tablespoon Leeks finely chopped
- 1 tablespoon Celery finely chopped
- ¼ cup Parmesan cheese grated
- Few sprigs Thyme
- 3 tablespoons Butter
- ½ cup carrot
- 1 Fennel bulb, roughly chopped
- 4 tablespoons Cream
- 2 tablespoons Truffle oil
- Salt and pepper, to taste
- 1 egg, beaten, for egg wash
- Use store bought pasta sheets to reduce effort.

Method:

For the mixture:

Take the whole lobster and steam it for 10-15 minutes in a stockpot or oven.

Remove all the meat from the shells, chop it and keep it aside to cool.

Sauté some finely chopped garlic, onion, leeks and celery in a pan until translucent. Add this to the lobster meat and mix it.

Add grated parmesan, chopped thyme, salt and pepper to the lobster mixture. The ravioli mixture is ready.

For the ravioli sauce:

Roast the lobster shells in a preheated oven at 370 F for about 30 minutes.

Take a stockpot and sauté some garlic, mirepoix and fennel in olive oil.

Add the roasted lobster shells and mix it with the mirepoix.

Add water to it. First, bring it to boil and then lower the heat and allow it simmer for 35-45 minutes.

Strain the stock using a medium fine meshed strainer. Discard the shells.

Transfer half of the lobster stock to a saucepot and reduce it until thickened. Add 3-4 tablespoons of fresh cream off the flame to make the sauce and adjust the seasonings. Serve this sauce with the ravioli.

Keep the rest of the stock separately, as this will be used to cook the ravioli.

For Ravioli:

Take a pasta sheet and lay it flat on a work surface or plate.

Cut out medium-large rounds with a cookie cutter.

Place a large tablespoon of the lobster mix on one of the pasta circles you've cut out. Carefully brush the edges of the circle with egg wash.

Place another pasta round on top of each one and press the edges of the circles together to seal. Make sure there are no air gaps for the filling to leak out from.

Heat the lobster stock up to cook the ravioli in. Heat to slightly less than a rolling boil. Drop ravioli in, a few at a time. Don't drop all in at once or the pasta will stick together. Cook till slightly al dente.

Transfer boiled raviolis to bowl and dress it with black truffle oil.

Heat the lobster sauce and pour on the serving dish.

Place the ravioli on the sauce and serve.

Drizzle some more sauce on top and garnish with optional herbs.

The Best Burger In New York

The episode where the gang goes out looking for that elusive burger is epic! Marshall's "This is no mere sandwich of grilled meat and toasted bread, Robin. This is God, speaking to us through food" truly spoke to me!

Serves: 2

Time: 1 hour

Ingredients

For the Patty:

- 2 cups Ground beef chuck
- 1 Egg
- 1 tablespoon Worcestershire sauce
- 1 teaspoon Mustard Dijon
- Salt To taste
- Pepper To taste
- 1 teaspoon Onion powder
- 1 teaspoon Onion powder
- 2 Burger buns
- 2 tbsp Softened butter
- 4 tbsp Mayonnaise
- 2 Cheddar cheese slices
- 2 tbsp Mustard sauce
- 2 Gherkins, sliced
- 6 Tomatoes slices
- Few Lettuce leaves

Method:

For hamburger patty: Take a large mixing bowl and add in the ground beef, egg, Worcestershire sauce, Dijon mustard, salt, onion powder, and pepper. Mix it until the meat mixture is smooth.

Divide the patty mixture to make two equal sized patties.

Gather the mixture and press firmly into patties using a ring mold of the size of the burger bun. Shape them just slightly larger than the buns you plan to use, to account for shrinkage during cooking.

Set the patties on a plate lined with parchment paper and refrigerate it till you cook it.

Preheat the grill or a skillet to medium heat and grill the patties for 3-4 minutes per side.

Place the cheese slice just a minute before the patty is cooked. Take the cooked patty from the griddle and keep it to rest until assembled.

Cut the burger bun into halves.

Brush some soft butter and toast the bun.

When crisp, apply mustard and mayonnaise to the buns on both sides.

Assemble the burger by placing the bottom half of the bun with lettuce leaves, sliced tomatoes, then the burger patty and gherkins. Season with some salt and pepper if required. Top it with the other half of the bun to close it.

Serve warm.

Gazola's Pizza

We all have that one pizza place that calls to us, right? And of course, Gazola's was that place for Marshall and Ted. It may not have been the pizza itself since it has been called a "filthy Mecca of spectacular if under cooked pizza", but more the emotional sentiment because that's where Ted and Marshall truly became brothers, more than friends!

Serves: 8

Time: 1 hour

Ingredients

For pizza dough:

- 2 cups Water (room temperature)
- 1 tbsp Sea salt
- 4 cups flour
- 1 tbsp yeast
- 2 tsp Sugar

For Pizza sauce:

- 1 cup Peeled tinned tomatoes
- Fresh Mozzarella cheese
- Few Leaves Basil leaves
- ¼ cup Olive Oil
- Salt, to taste
- Pepper, to taste
- 1 tsp Oregano

Method:

For the Pizza dough:

Take a large pan or working surface and put flour on it.

Make a well in the middle and add the salt, sugar, yeast and add little water to it.

Mix it all to dissolve it and activate the yeast.

Cover it with flour and keep it for 1-2 minutes.

Now add the remaining water to the flour to make a firm dough.

Add the olive oil and knead the dough again. The dough should not be very soft.

Keep the dough in a bowl, apply some oil to keep it moist and cover it with cling film.

Let it proof for 30-40 minutes at room temperature till it gets double in size.

After the dough gets double in size, knead it again and portion it into small balls as required.

Place the dough balls on a plate, apply some oil and cover it with cling wrap.

Keep this dough refrigerated till you make the pizzas.

For the pizza sauce:

Blitz a cup of tinned Italian tomatoes in a blender and transfer it to a bowl. We don't want a very fine puree but a coarse one.

Add a teaspoon of dried oregano, salt, pepper and a tablespoon of olive oil and mix it. Check seasonings and the pizza sauce is ready.

Making the pizza:

Take the pizza dough ball and roll into the desired size with your hands or rolling pin.

Smear the pizza sauce on the base.

Tear the mozzarella cheese with hands and put on top of the sauce.

Place the pizza on the pizza bat and bake it in the pizza oven for 10 minutes at 400 F

Take it out from the oven, garnish with fresh basil leaves and drizzle some olive oil.

Cut it into slices and serve hot.

Hummus with Veggie Sticks

This was part of the menu that Lily served at the eventful Thanksgiving with her father and the bees! Simple to make and very healthy for that diet you've meant to go on for ages!

Serves: 4

Time: 20 mins

Ingredients

For hummus

- 1 cup Chickpeas, from a tin
- 4 small Garlic cloves
- Juice of 2 Lemons
- Salt, to taste
- 2 tbsp Tahini paste
- ¼ cup olive oil

For vegetables

- Vegetable, all cut into sticks
- 1 Carrot
- 1 Cucumber
- 1 Celery
- 2 Bell Peppers, assorted colors

Method:

Cut the vegetables into sticks and keep it in the refrigerator.

Wash the chickpeas in cold running water and strain it.

Roast garlic in a pan on medium low flame in olive oil till light brown and fragrant.

In a food processor, add the boiled chickpeas, tahini paste, salt and garlic, extra virgin olive oil and blend into a fine paste. If required add more oil and a few tablespoons of water.

Finish it with lemon juice. Check the seasoning.

Drizzle some olive oil on top of the hummus, to prevent it from drying. Transfer to a serving bowl.

Serve cold with the vegetable sticks.

Nachos with Tomato Salsa

This one's quite the staple, isn't it! But instead of buying gross store-bought salsa, try making your own! It's fresher and the zing in it absolutely surpasses any store-bought mushy salsa!

Serves: 4

Time: 45 mins

Ingredients

- 5 Ripe tomatoes, finely chopped
- 2 Jalapenos or green chili, finely chopped
- 1 onion, finely chopped
- Juice of 2 Lemons
- Salt, to taste
- ¼ cup olive oil 1 sprig Cilantro, chopped
- A big handful of Corn chips

Method:

Wash the ripe tomatoes and cut into quarters. Deseed them and chop it and place it in a bowl.

Finely chopped the green chili, onion, coriander leaves and garlic. Add them to chopped tomatoes.

Squeeze the juice of one or two lemon and add it to the mixture.

Add salt and olive oil to the mixture and mix it thoroughly. Adjust the seasonings and tanginess of the salsa according to required taste.

Keep the salsa refrigerated for at least 30 minutes before serving to release the juices and enhance the taste.

Place the nachos on the plate and serve the chilled tomato salsa in small bowls.

Mac and Cheese

What is an American sitcom with a healthy serving of Mac and Cheese? This recipe down here is the basic version. Feel free to jazz it up with bacon or even truffles if you're in the mood to splurge!

Serves: 4

Time: 30 mins

Ingredients

For the sauce

- 2 cups Milk
- ½ cup Flour
- ½ cup Butter
- 2 Bay leaves
- 3 Peppercorn, whole
- 4 tbsp Cheddar cheese
- 4 tbsp Gruyere cheese
- 2 tbsp Parmesan cheese
- 1 cup Macaroni dry
- ½ cup Cream
- 1 tbsp Mustard
- Salt, To taste
- Pepper, To taste

Method:

Put the milk, onion, bay leaves and whole peppercorns into a large pan, then bring to the boil and simmer for few minutes on low flame to infuse all the flavors.

Strain into a jug and discard the flavorings.

In a separate large pan, melt the butter over a medium heat. Add the flour and cook gently, stirring, for about 30 seconds, then remove from the heat. Gradually beat in the hot milk, then return the pan to the heat and bring the mixture to the boil while stirring. Lower the heat, then simmer stirring now and then till the macaroni is blanched.

Meanwhile, cook the macaroni in a large pan of boiling salted water for 10 minutes till al dente. Drain the pasta and transfer into a container.

Preheat the oven to 200°C.

Take the sauce off the heat, then stir in all of the grated cheddar and gruyere cheese, 1 tbsp mustard and the cream, then season with salt and white pepper.

Pour and stir in the sauce into the cooked macaroni. The mixture should be nicely moist. Spoon into a buttered deep baking dish.

Sprinkle the grated parmesan cheese over the macaroni, then bake for 10-12 minutes until golden and bubbling hot.

Serve hot with some more grated cheese on top.

Pumpkin Risotto

The trick with cooking risotto is to add the stock in parts. Adding the stock in batches helps to create a creamy starch. Wait until the rice has absorbed all the stock before you add the next lot!

Serves: 2

Time: 40 mins

Ingredients

- ½ cup Pumpkin, diced
- 1 cup Risotto rice
- 2 cups Vegetable stock, or as required
- 2 tbsp Onion
- 4 tbsp Olive oil
- 1 sprig Thyme
- 1 tbsp Garlic
- 3 tbsp Parmesan cheese grated
- 2 tbsp Butter
- Salt and white pepper to taste
- Parsley, chopped, to garnish

Method:

Heat some olive oil in a pan and sauté the onion and garlic till translucent.

Add the rice and keep on sautéing till the rice also turns translucent.

Add whole thyme sprig and add some stock to the pan. Keep stirring.

Cook the risotto by adding the vegetable stock little by little till it gets all absorbed.

Add the diced pumpkin also to the rice half-way and cook it till the pumpkin is tender and rice is al dente. It should take around 20-25 minutes.

Switch off the flame, add seasonings, cheese, butter and parsley and give a nice mix till the risotto gets creamy. Adjust the consistency by adding some stock. Also, check the seasoning.

Serve hot with some more grated parmesan cheese on top.

Marshall's Cheese Board

Poor Marshall, no one wanted his cheese! This cheeseboard is a guideline for your next party platter… Feel free to change the types of crackers and the fruit paste.

Serves: 6

Time: 15 mins

Ingredients

- 1 wedge, Gouda cheese
- 1 wedge, Manchego cheese
- 1 wedge Cheddar cheese
- 1 wedge Emmenthal cheese
- 1 small wheel Brie cheese, cut into triangles
- ½ cup Apricots dried
- 4 Prunes
- 5-6 Marinated Olives
- 2-3 tbsp Fig compote/any preserve
- 1 bunch Fresh grapes
- Walnuts, to taste
- 8 Cheese crackers

Method:

Using a cheese knife slice all the Gouda, Manchego, Cheddar and Emmenthal cheese and cut the brie into 8 triangles.

Take a wooden board or a platter and arrange all the cheese slices overlapping each other symmetrically.

Place dried apricots, prunes and walnuts in between the cheeses placed on the cheese board.

Arrange some fresh grapes and cheese cracker biscuits on the sides of the cheese board.

Put some fig compote or any preserves in a small bowl and serve on the side of the cheese board.

Serve it at room temperature along with wine.

🌶 Stir Fried Chicken Noodles

The gang is always eating Chinese takeout on the show, but we never really get to see what they eat! This is my interpretation of Chinese takeout, and I can promise you it is as good as any takeout can get!

Serves: 2

Time: 30 mins

Ingredients

- 3 ounces Noodles
- 1 Chicken breast, julienned
- 1 Onion, julienned
- 1 Carrot, julienned
- ½ cup Cabbage, julienned
- 1 Capsicum Green, julienned
- 1 Capsicum yellow, julienned
- 1 Capsicum Red, julienned
- 1 tsp Chopped garlic
- 1/2 tsp Chopped ginger
- 2 tbsp Spring onion, chopped
- 1 tsp Soy Sauce
- 1 tbsp Vinegar
- Salt, To taste
- White pepper powder, To taste
- Chicken stock powder/cubes, optional, to taste
- 1 tbsp Sesame oil, to drizzle

Method:

Cooking noodles: Fill a pot with enough water and bring to a boil.

Season with salt, and add the noodles to it, and cook as per packet instructions.

Drain the noodles using a colander. Add 1 tbsp of oil to the noodles and coat well to prevent them from turning sticky.

Heat oil in a large wok or pan on a high flame and sauté garlic, onions and chicken for 30 seconds by tossing it vigorously. Next add in carrots, capsicum and cabbage. Fry it for 1 to 2 minutes until the vegetables are partially cooked, yet crunchy.

Add boiled noodles to the pan. Lower the heat and add light and dark soy, vinegar, chicken broth powder, salt and pepper to taste.

Increase the heat to high and toss all the vegetables, noodles and condiments for about 1 to 2 minutes.

Check the seasoning, drizzle some sesame oil and give a nice toss

Garnish with spring onions and serve hot.

Chicken Dumplings

To be fair, I wouldn't mind if my apartment turned into a House of Dumplings, as long as I got a free lifetime supply of chicken dumplings! But since that isn't going to happen to me anytime soon, so I made my own recipe to keep my dumpling craving satisfied!

Serves: 2

Time: 1.5 hours

Ingredients:

Stuffing:

- 1 cup Chicken mince
- 4 tbsp Chopped onion
- 1tbsp Chopped garlic
- ½ tsp Chopped ginger
- 1 tbsp Light soy
- 1 tbsp Sesame oil
- 1 tbsp Chopped spring onion
- Salt, to taste
- Black pepper powder, to taste

Dipping sauce:

- 2 Cloves garlic, minced
- 1 tsp Ginger fresh chopped
- 3 tbsp Light soy sauce
- 2 tbsp Chinese rice vinegar
- 2 tsp Sesame oil
- 1 tsp chili oil
- 1 sprig Scallions chopped
- ½ tsp sesame seeds, optional
- Salt and pepper To taste
- Ready-made dumpling wrappers

Method:

Filling:

Take a large steel bowl and put chicken mince in the bowl. Add chopped onions, garlic, ginger, soya sauce, sesame oil, spring onions, salt and pepper as per recipe.

Take a rubber spatula and mix it all together till all the flavors are incorporated. Keep it refrigerated for about 20-25 mins to allow it to firm up.

Folding the dumpling:

Scoop about 1 tablespoon (or less, so you can easily fold the dumpling) of filling and place it in the center of the wrapper.

Hold the dumpling with one hand and fold into half-moon shape and start sealing the edges by folding and making small pleats with the other hand.

Make sure to pinch the edges together to seal the dumplings so that it doesn't break and hold their shape while steaming.

Place the dumplings on the working surface and work on the rest of the dough in the same manner until all the dumplings are folded and ready to be steamed.

To steam dumplings, prepare the steamer by adding 2" (5cm) water to the steamer. Heat it over medium heat until steaming.

Place the dumplings onto the steaming rack, at least one finger apart each other (the dumplings will expand after cooking).

Steam covered for 10 minutes until the dumplings are completely cooked through.

Dipping sauce:

In a small bowl, combine the garlic, ginger, soy sauce, vinegar, sesame oil, scallions and 1 teaspoon of the hot chili oil. Whisk until well combined. Sprinkle sesame seeds, if using

Adjust seasonings and serve dipping sauce with hot steamed dumplings.

Buffalo Wings

Who can forget that episode where they taped the Super Bowl, and everyone avoided seeing the results until they could watch it together! These buffalo wings are from that episode, but I won't mind if you gorge on them all the time!

Serves: 3

Time: 40 mins

Ingredients

- 12 Chicken wings
- 1 ½ cup plain flour
- 1 tsp Garlic powder
- 1 tsp Onion powder
- 1 tsp Cayenne pepper powder
- 2 Eggs
- 3 cups Oil for deep-frying
- Salt To taste
- Pepper To taste

For the sauce:

- ½ cup Melted butter
- ½ cup Hot sauce (store-bought)
- 2 tbsp White vinegar
- 4 tbsp Honey
- ¼ cup Ranch sauce (store-bought)

Method:

Marinate the chicken wings with some salt, pepper, garlic powder, onion powder and cayenne pepper in a large bowl.

Crack 2 eggs and mix it to the chicken wings which will help to coat the flour.

Place the flour in a separate bowl and taking each marinated wing, dredge it in flour and keep aside on a plate.

Heat oil in a pan until hot and deep fry the chicken wings in batches, turning as needed until crisp. It should take about 10- 12 minutes on medium heat.

Take it out from the oil and drain on paper towels.

For Buffalo sauce:

In a small saucepan, whisk together hot sauce, white vinegar and honey. Bring to simmer then stir in melted butter. Cook until slightly reduced, about 2 minutes.

Transfer deep fried wings to a bowl and toss with buffalo sauce until completely coated.

Serve chicken wings hot with ranch sauce.

Sumbitches Cookie

Finally! The moment when Lily meets the mother! These cookies are fantastic and will be the perfect opening for a conversation, especially with what they are called! Easy to make and amazing with or without a glass of milk!

Serves: 2

Time: 1 hour

Ingredients

- 6 tbsp Butter
- ½ cup Brown sugar
- ¾ cup Chunky Peanut Butter
- 2 Whole eggs
- ½ tsp Baking powder
- 1 tsp Vanilla essence
- 1 cup Plain flour
- ¾ cup Chocolate chips
- ¾ cup Caramel bits

Method:

Preheat your oven to 350 F and line a baking tray with parchment paper.

Beat butter and sugar until light and fluffy. It should take about 5-7 minutes. The butter will change to a pale color once done.

Add the peanut butter and continue to beat on a medium speed, until fully incorporated.

Add the eggs, one at the time, beating until combined. Don't forget to scrape the sides of the bowl.

Whisk in the vanilla extract.

Sieve flour, baking powder and salt into a separate bowl.

Fold the flour mix in the butter and sugar mix using a spatula. Mix lightly until incorporated.

Fold in the chocolate chips and caramel bits.

Using an ice-cream scooper, scoop out the cookie dough, shape into a ball and then slightly flatten. Place on the cookie sheet, about 2 inches apart.

Bake for 8-9 minutes until an even brown.

Remove from the oven and allow to cool down to room temperature on a wire rack.

Victoria's Cupcakes/Cake

Who can forget the gorgeous Victoria! I mean, for a few episodes, I actually thought she was the mother! And because I'm such a baker at heart, I guess I had an extra soft spot for her character. Anyway, try this cupcake recipe and have everyone swooning over them, just like Ted used to swoon over Victoria's cupcakes!

Serves: 12

Time: 1.5 hours

Ingredients

- 1 cup plain flour
- ¾ cup brown sugar
- 1 tsp baking soda
- 1 tsp salt
- ½ cup oil, (use something with a neutral flavor)
- 8 tbsp cocoa powder
- ½ cup hot water
- ½ cup buttermilk (or ½ cup milk with 1 tbsp vinegar added)
- Instant coffee 1tbsp
- Vanilla extract 1 tsp
- 1 egg

Frosting

- 2 cups Chocolate chips
- 1 cup Heavy Cream
- A pinch of salt

Method:

Preheat your oven to 320 F.

In a bowl, mix flour, sugar, cocoa, baking soda and salt.

In another bowl, mix the egg, buttermilk, oil and vanilla essence.

Once combined, add to the flour mixture and stir to make a batter.

Add coffee to hot water and stir this mix carefully into the batter. The batter will be runny.

Line the baking tray with cupcake wrappers and fill 3/4th with batter.

Bake for 15 minutes or till done. Check doneness by inserting a skewer into the middle. The skewer should come out clean. Leave on counter to cool.

For the frosting, heat cream in a saucepan till boiling.

Place chocolate chips and salt in a bowl and pour cream over the chocolate.

Let the heat of the cream melt the chocolate. This should take 5 minutes at the most.

Stir gently to combine. Do not whisk or aerate, we don't want bubbles in the frosting.

Place in the fridge to cool down completely.

Once cold, whisk this mix till stiff peak.

Once the cupcakes are cooled to room temperature, add the frosting in a piping bag with a nozzle and pipe on top of the cupcakes.

Carrot Cupcakes

This Carrot Cupcake recipe is Victoria inspired through and through. Make this to wow everyone around. The silky frosting pairs really well with the cupcake itself and makes for an absolute stunner.

Serves: 12

Time: 1 hour

Ingredients

- 1 cup pecan nuts, chopped
- ¾ cup brown sugar
- ½ tsp Ginger powder
- 1 cup oil
- 2 Eggs
- ½ tsp Baking Powder
- ½ tsp Salt
- ½ tsp Cinnamon powder
- ¼ tsp Nutmeg powder
- ¼ tsp Clove powder
- 1 cup Grated carrots, excess juice squeezed out
- 1 tsp Baking Soda
- 1 tsp Vanilla essence
- 1 cup plain flour

Frosting

- 1 cups cream cheese
- ½ cup softened butter
- 2 cups powdered sugar
- a pinch, salt
- 1-2 tbsp cream/milk
- 1 ½ tsp Vanilla essence

Method:

Preheat the oven to 350 F.

Toast the pecans and allow to cool for 10-15 minutes.

Grease a muffin tin or use muffin liners.

Combine all the dry ingredients in one bowl. This includes the flour, grated carrots, nuts, sugar, baking soda, salt, baking powder and the spices. Reserve a few pecans for garnish

Combine the wet ingredients (oil and eggs) in another bowl.

Pour the wet ingredients into the dry ingredients and, using a rubber spatula or wooden spoon, fold the ingredients together until just combined.

Pour/spoon the batter evenly into the muffin tins. Bake for 15 mins or until a skewer inserted in the center comes out clean. Chill completely before frosting.

For the frosting: In a large bowl, beat the cream cheese, vanilla essence, salt and butter together until smooth.

Add the icing sugar in batches, until frosting is smooth. Beat until completely combined and creamy.

Adjustments: Add more sugar if frosting is too thin, cream if frosting is too thick, or an extra pinch of salt if frosting is too sweet. Frosting should be soft, but not runny.

Chill the frosting for 10-15 minutes to firm up slightly.

Frost the top of cooled cupcakes and use the remaining pecans to garnish.

Chocolate Brownie with Strawberries

Would Lily and Victoria be impressed? I think so! This recipe is foolproof, I mean, there's nothing you can do to turn this into a fail. Use good quality cocoa powder to impress everyone!

Serves: 5

Time: 2 hours

Ingredients

- 1 cup plain flour
- 1 tsp baking powder
- ½ tsp salt
- 2 cups castor sugar
- 4 eggs
- 2 tsp Vanilla Essence
- ¼ cup Cocoa powder
- 4 tbsp milk
- 4 tbsp oil
- ½ cup melted butter

Chocolate ganache:

- 2 cups chocolate chips, dark or milk
- 1 cup heavy cream
- 2 cup fresh strawberries, halved

Method:

1.Preheat the oven to 320 F.

Line the bottom of an 8-inch (20cm) pan with the parchment paper hanging over the sides.

2. Combine the melted butter and oil in a bowl or the bowl of a stand mixer.

3. Add the sugar to a large mixer bowl and beat together into a paste.

4. Add eggs one at a time, beating until mostly combined after each addition, on a low speed, till light and fluffy.

5. Beat in the vanilla extract.

6. Sift the dry ingredients together in another bowl (flour, cocoa, baking powder, salt)

7. Carefully fold the dry mix into the egg mix.

8. Slowly add the milk and beat until combined.

9. Bake for 25 mins or until a skewer inserted comes out clean.

10. Remove from the oven and allow to cool completely. Leave the brownie in the tin, but loosen from sides.

11. While the brownie cools, make the chocolate ganache. Add the chocolate chips to a bowl.

12. Heat the cream until it begins to boil. Pour the boiling cream over the chocolate chips.

Let the mix sit for a few minutes, then gently mix with a spatula until smooth, with no lumps. Set aside to cool.

13. Once the brownie is cool, place the strawberries, flat side down.

14. Pour the cooled ganache over the brownie, covering the strawberries. Let it set in the fridge.

15. Once completely chilled, hold the paper and lift out gently. Cut into squares and serve.

Thanksgiving Turkey

Be it the Erikson house, or Lily's parties or even Ted's attempt at the TurTurkeyKey, a well-roasted Turkey is the centerpiece to any Thanksgiving celebration. Try this easy recipe to bedazzle your friends and family!

Serves: 4

Time: 3.5 hours

Ingredients

- 1 fresh turkey, 10-12 pounds, cleaned with giblets removed
- 1 stick butter
- 1 lemon, halved
- 4-5 cloves of garlic, crushed
- 1 small bunch parsley, chopped
- 2 sprigs rosemary, chopped
- 1 small bunch parsley, chopped
- Flaky Salt & pepper, to taste
- Oil to drizzle over

For the Stuffing

- 2 small onions, halved
- 1 head of garlic, halved through the middle
- 2-3 small sprigs rosemary

Method:

1. Preheat your oven to 450 Fahrenheit and take out the turkey from the refrigerator so that it may reach room temperature.

2. Prepare the garlic butter by combining the butter, garlic and herbs in a bowl. If using salted butter, lower the amount of salt you add. Squeeze the juice of the lemon into the butter mix but don't discard the lemon.

3. Whisk ingredients together to form this fragrant garlic herb butter.

4. Prepare your turkey by patting it dry with some paper towels. Place into a heavy bottomed roasting pan that is deep enough to hold the turkey drippings. Thoroughly season the inside of the turkey.

5. Gently separate the skin of the bird from the breast area by pushing your fingers underneath.

6. Rub the butter under the skin and on top, taking care to cover every bit of the turkey.

7. Stuff the cavity with the onions, squeezed lemon, head of garlic and rosemary. Tie the legs together with kitchen string.

8. Drizzle the oil generously over the turkey and sprinkle a little more salt on top to help crisp up the skin.

9. Bake for 20 mins at 430 F.

10. Baste the turkey with the melted butter in the tray every 20 minutes or so.

11. Lower the temperature to 350-degree F and bake for another 2 ½ hours. Continue to baste so keep the turkey from drying out.

7-layer Erickson Inspired Salad

Before you can ask, no, this version doesn't have gummy bears and funyuns in it. This one is an actually edible layered salad that I think Lily would be proud of!

Serves: 4

Time: 2 hours

Ingredients

- 2 cups Iceberg or Romaine lettuce, chopped
- ½ cup red onion, chopped
- 6 hard boiled eggs, halved
- ½ cup peas
- ½ cup red bell pepper, chopped
- ½ cup cucumber, chopped
- 1 cup mayonnaise
- 1 cup bacon, chopped
- ½ cup cheddar, shredded
- Salt and pepper to taste

Method:

Crispen the bacon in a pan or hot oven. Leave it to cool at room temperature.

Rinse and dry lettuce using a lettuce spinner.

Chop all the vegetables, lettuce slice the eggs and grate the cheese. Keep them aside.

Assemble the salad: Take a trifle bowl or any clear glass serving bowl or jar and put a layer of lettuce leaves. Sprinkle with salt and pepper.

Top with layers of onion, hard boiled eggs, peas, bell pepper, and cucumber.

Top it with mayonnaise spread over top of the salad in a thick layer.

Top it with shredded cheese and crumbled crispy bacon.

Refrigerate for an hour and serve chilled.

🌿 Baked Gouda in Potato Skin

I can't vouch for the taste of Marshall's Gouda, but I can definitely tell you that this baked Gouda in Potato Skins recipe is absolutely smashing! There's no way that you can skip on this one, that's for sure!

Serves: 2

Time: 30 mins

Ingredients

- 4 Medium Russet Potatoes, scrubbed clean
- 1 stick butter
- ¼ cup milk
- Salt and pepper to taste
- 4 cloves garlic, minced
- 1 spring onion, chopped
- ½ cup gouda cheese
- ¼ cup Bacon or Chorizo, chopped

Method:

Scrub and wash the potatoes and put it a pot for boiling in salted water till 80% cooked.

Carefully in half, lengthwise.

Scoop out the potatoes using a spoon by keeping the skin intact to make the shells.

Mash the potato scooped out with butter, milk, salt, pepper and garlic.

When the mash is completely smooth, stir in the chopped green onion and 1/4 cup of the gouda cheese.

Place shells on a lightly greased baking tray and stuff it with the mashed potatoes mix. Top with chopped bacon or chorizo and more grated gouda cheese.

Bake for 5-10 minutes in the oven at 350 F until cheese is melted and bacon/chorizo is crispy.

Garnish with chopped spring onions.

Serve hot.

Salmon Sushi

Sushi in New York? Well, if it's good enough for the gang, it's sure good enough for us! This one is a simple salmon and avocado sushi that you can easily make at home!

Serves: 2

Time: 40 mins

Ingredients

- 1 cup Sushi rice
- 2 cups water
- 1.5 oz sushi vinegar
- 3-4 nori sheets

Filling:

- Cucumber batons
- Avocado slices
- Sashimi grade salmon, cut into sticks

Accompaniments:

- Soya sauce, pickled ginger and wasabi paste

Method:

Cooking sushi rice:

Thoroughly rinse the rice in cold water and discard the liquid. Pour the water into a pot, add the rice and bring to the boil for 3 minutes. Then simmer for about 5-10 minutes, or until all the moisture is absorbed.

Check frequently to make sure it doesn't stick to the bottom of the pot and burn. Remove from heat.

Pour into a large bowl that isn't too deep and allow it to cool. Gently pour in the sushi vinegar and mix until the rice has cooled down.

To make the sushi rolls:

Lay a bamboo mat in front of you. Place a sheet of nori on top.

Slightly dampen your fingers and scoop some rice on the sheet of nori. Pat down the rice gently, leaving a little gap towards the top of the nori sheet. The rice layer should be thin, since you will be rolling this.

Place the cucumber, avocado, salmon in a line along the bottom edge of the rice. Lift the mat with your thumbs, and while holding the filling as close as possible, tightly roll the sushi mat away from you, like you would with a cinnamon roll. Press to seal.

Slice into pieces just before you intend to serve/eat the sushi.

Serve with the traditional accompaniments: soy sauce, wasabi paste, and pickled ginger.

Meatball Sub sandwiches

Anyone remember the exploding sub incident? Lol! That was such a good episode, don't you think? I only wish I was at good at pranking people as Barney was!

Serves 1

Time: 1 hour

Ingredients

For the meatballs

- 1 lb beef mince, room temperature
- 1 tbsp onion powder
- 1 tsp garlic powder
- 2 tsp mixed dried herbs
- 2 tbsp BBQ sauce
- 1 tbsp tomato ketchup
- 1 egg
- ½ cup breadcrumbs
- 1 medium sized onion, finely chopped
- Salt and Pepper, to season

Other ingredients

- 3 tbsp oil
- 1 bread roll
- 1 ½ cups pizza sauce
- ½ cup shredded cheese (I use mozzarella)

Optional: A few leaves of Fresh Basil

Method:

This will make quite a few meatballs, but we will only use 3 per sub. These freeze well, just in case you can't eat them all in one sitting!

1. Preheat the oven to 350 degrees F.

2. To make the meatballs, add all the ingredients to a big bowl and mix till properly combined. Do not overwork the meat.

3. Rest for about 15 minutes and then roll into small balls.

4. Add the oil to a pan over a medium heat. Gently place meatballs in the pan and fry for about 1-1.5 minutes on each side, depending on the size of the meatballs.

5. Once golden brown, lower the heat and add the pizza sauce to the pan. Simmer for another 7-10 minutes or until the meatballs are soft and cooked throughout. Remove from heat.

6. Slit the bread roll but not all the way through.

7. Add 3-4 meatballs per bread roll as per your liking.

8. Add the cheese on top carefully and place on an oven tray.

9. Take out as soon as cheese has melted, usually in a couple of minutes, depending on your oven.

10. Sprinkle the fresh basil leaves, if you've got any and serve hot!

Beef Teppanyaki

If you ask me, I think Barney is responsible for half the gags in the show… I mean, imagine mastering Teppanyaki skills just to win a bet! But um, would you bet against Barney in the first place?

Serves: 2

Time: 30 mins

Ingredients

- 14 oz Beef sirloin
- ½ cup Shiitake Mushroom, sliced
- ½ cup King Oyster Mushroom, sliced
- ½ cup onion, sliced
- ½ cup bell peppers, sliced
- Refined oil 1 tbsp
- Salt and Pepper, to taste

For the Teppanyaki sauce:

- 1 tbsp Sake
- 2 tbsp Mirin
- 2 tbsp Sugar
- 4 tbsp Soy sauce
- ½ tsp Chopped ginger
- ½ tsp minced garlic
- 1 tbsp Sesame oil
- 1 tsp Toasted white sesame seeds

Method:

1. For the teppanyaki Sauce, heat sake and mirin in a small saucepan on a medium flame and let the alcohol evaporate for 1-2 minutes.

2. Now add the sugar to the pan and whisk to combine.

3. Add soy sauce, chopped ginger, chopped garlic, sesame oil and sesame seeds.

4. Whisk together and cook on low heat for a minute.

5. Turn off the heat and let it cool down to room temperature.

6. Keep aside to be served along with the meat and vegetables.

Teppanyaki:

1. Preheat an Electric griddle to 370 F and season with oil.

2. Divide the griddle into 2 spaces: one side for vegetables and the other for meat.

3. Add in the sliced mushrooms, onion and bell peppers on one side and season with salt and pepper.

4. Cook the beef on the other side according to your preference for doneness.

5. Season it with salt and pepper.

6. Arrange the beef and mushroom on a platter.

7. Serve with Teppanyaki sauce on the side

Vegan Spring rolls

This is another recipe from Lily's thanksgiving party, the one with the bees… You know, the one where Ted got into an argument with Garrison Cootes, even though it was Barney who ate all the spring rolls! Anyway, you're going to love these spring rolls, vegan or not!

Serves: 2

Time: 1 hour

Ingredients

- 1 cup Carrots, finely shredded
- 1 cup Onion, sliced
- 1 tbsp Ginger, minced
- 1 tbsp Garlic, minced
- 1 cup Cabbage, shredded
- 1 cup Bell peppers, julienned
- 2 Spring onions, chopped
- Salt and Pepper to taste
- 1 stock cube (vegetable)
- 4 tbsp oil, to cook filling
- 2 tsp soy sauce
- 1 tsp Vinegar
- 7 Spring roll sheets
- Oil, to deep fry
- Sweet chili sauce, to dip

Method:

1. Heat 4 tbsp oil in a wok or non-stick pan.

2. Add in the onions, ginger, garlic and lightly fry on medium heat for 2 to 3 minutes.

3. Now add in the carrot, cabbage and capsicum and cook on a high heat for 3- 4 minutes till the vegetables are crisp, but not fully cooked.

4. Lower the heat. Season it with salt, pepper, vinegar, light soy sauce.

5. Mix well and cook for a couple of minutes on medium heat.

6. Check the seasonings, finish with chopped spring onions.

7. Take the mixture off the heat. Allow it to cool it at room temperature.

8. Take a sheet of the spring roll pastry and spread a spoonful of mixture towards the lower end. Leave the end of the sheet free to fold over the filling and roll.

9. Close the ends of the sheet from the bottom, fold over both sides, securing the mixture inside, thus tightly rolling it towards the opposite end to seal it. You can use some water as an adhesive too.

10. Heat oil in a deep pot or in a deep fryer.

11. Fry the spring rolls, till golden brown and crisp.

12. Serve hot with sweet chili sauce.

The Robin Scherbatsky

Marshall might have originally created this, but it was named after Robin… To be fair, I've always wondered why Robin ordered this drink if she was a scotch person. Anyway, go ahead and enjoy!

Serves: 1

Time: 5 mins

Ingredients

- ½ shot coconut rum
- 1 shot Peach Schnapps
- 1 shot Vanilla vodka
- 1 shot strawberry cream liqueur
- ½ cup Cranberry juice
- ¼ cup Sugar
- 5-6 Maraschino cherries
- Whipped cream, optional

Method:

1. Blend all the ingredients and leave out the cherries in a mixer grinder.

2. Pour the cocktail in the hurricane glass. Top with whipped cream if using and garnish with cherries.

The Stinson's Hangover Fixer Elixir

I love Barney! And I absolutely love the character development for him! While I have left out the Funyuns, this recipe is an absolute winner! I dare you to tell me I'm wrong!

Serves: 1

Time: 5 mins

Ingredients

- 1 cup Mountain Dew
- 1 banana
- 1 tbsp Lemon Juice
- 1-inch Ginger, crushed
- 3-4 leaves mint
- A splash of sugar syrup

Method:

Blend all the ingredients together.

Pour over crushed ice into a glass.

Thankstini

All you need at Thanksgiving is a Thankstini and some TurTurkeyKey! No kidding, this drink is so delicious, Barney would totally approve of the changes, aka, no bouillon cube!

Serves: 1

Time: 5 mins

Ingredients

- 1 shot Dry gin
- 1 shot Port wine
- 1 tbsp Maple syrup
- 1 tbsp Lemon juice
- ½ cup Cranberry juice
- Cranberry skewer, for garnish
- Fresh sage or rosemary to garnish

Method:

1. Add all the ingredients except the garnishes, with some ice cubes to a cocktail shaker.

2. Shake for 15 seconds and double strain into a martini glass.

3. Crush sage/rosemary slightly to release its flavor and place it in the drink.

4. Garnish with fresh cranberries on a skewer and serve chilled.

The "Thank You, Linus"

We all need a Linus in our lives, am I right? This one's dedicated to Linus and I'm sure Lily won't mind! Thank you, Linus, even though you're slipping!

Serves: 1

Time: 5 mins

Ingredients

- 1 shot gin
- 2 shots tonic water
- 1 tbsp lime juice
- 1 lime slice, to garnish
- 1 sprig rosemary, to garnish

Method:

1. Add gin and tonic water plus lime juice to an ice-filled cocktail shaker.

2. Next, shake well and pour it into an ice filled glass.

3. Garnish with a slice of lime and rosemary.

Marshall's Self-Love Daiquiri

Okay, I admit. Marshall and Daiquiris are pretty epic! Imagine being so drunk that you want to make out with yourself! Anyway, try this Strawberry Daiquiri and stay away from mirrors!

Serves: 1

Time: 5 mins

Ingredients

- 1 shot, Coconut Rum
- 1 ½ tbsp lemon/lime juice
- 2 tbsp Sugar syrup
- 7-8 frozen Strawberries
- 1 sprig of mint, to garnish
- 1 slice lime, to garnish

Method:

1. Blend all ingredients together.

2. Pour into a daiquiri glass and garnish with Mint.

The Yellow Umbrella

Of course, this is inspired by the mother! Tracy Moseby was a breath of fresh air and the culmination of so much anticipation. This drink is dedicated to her yellow umbrella and her version of La Vie En Rose.

Serves: 1

Time: 5 mins

Ingredients

- 1 shot Tequila
- 1 shot Lemonade
- 1 shot Ginger Ale
- 1 shot sparkling water
- 1 tsp sugar syrup
- Lemon slices, to garnish

Method:

1. Combine all ingredients in a shaker.

2. Pour into a glass filled with ice.

3. Garnish with a lemon slice.

Robin's "But-um" shots

This is probably one of the most famous drinking games I know of! Robin is so famous for saying, "but, umm" that you can make a drinking game out of it and get super drunk! Try these shots but not with HIMYM on… LOL!

Serves: 1

Time: 5 mins

Ingredients

- 1-part Peach Schnapps
- ½ part Vanilla vodka
- ½ part Pineapple Juice

Method:

1. In a cocktail shaker, combine all the ingredients with some ice cubes.

2. Shake well.

3. Strain into a shot glass.

Conclusion

Well, there you have it. A collection of my favorite foods and dishes were mentioned in one of my favorite shows. How I Met Your Mother is a heartwarming, genuinely funny show, and I hope the dishes you create after reading through this cookbook will give rise to equally heartwarming stories and conversations in your life.

There is nothing like food to unite people and give them a common place to start! How I Met Your Mother brought together five people who were completely opposite characters, who together made for a very vibrant tapestry.

Food is quite similar in that sense. Good food unites people, despite their backgrounds and culture. It brings people together and gives them a reason to start a conversation. Look around you, and start a conversation with someone about food… We'd love to hear from you about how food has changed your life and the memories you associate with this wonderful sitcom.

Thanks for reading and trying out these dishes! You are legend-wait-for-it-dary!

Author's Afterthoughts

It's incredible to think that I hesitated to publish my book, thinking that it wouldn't get as much as a single attention from anyone. But here we are. You all have bought and accepted this book, and it means more than you can ever imagine. So, here's me asking for one more favor. I would love to know your thoughts on this book. Your feedback will mean a lot to me and help others who are searching for the right book.

Thanks,

Dan Babel

About the Author

From humble beginnings in a little town in Florida to the big stage, Dan Babel had always known that his path included a lot of food. As a child, he was always in the kitchen with his mother and grandmother. Most times, it was to see what he could grab when no one was looking. However, he was also attracted to what he saw as "magic." He wondered how something as white and simple as flour could create the delicious cakes he could never let go of. His curiosity led him from just eating the meals to being a part of the cooking process.

As a natural, Dan realized that it didn't take long for him to learn even the most complex of recipes. It was inevitable that he would head to culinary school just after he completed high school. After his graduation, Dan worked with a team of chefs whose specialty was traditional Asian dishes. Thanks to the skills learned here, he went on to open up his restaurant. It has been close to a decade, and it keeps getting better.